S0-CFF-148

LIFE IN THE MIDDLE AGES™

WEAPONS AND WARCRAFT

MARGAUX BAUM AND
PAUL HILLIAM

rosen publishing's
rosen
central

NEW YORK

Published in 2017 by The Rosen Publishing Group, Inc.
29 East 21st Street, New York, NY 10010

First Edition

Library of Congress Cataloging-in-Publication Data

Names: Baum, Margaux. | Hilliam, Paul.
Title: Weapons and warcraft / Margaux Baum and Paul Hilliam, first edition.
Description: New York : Rosen Publishing, 2017. | Series: Life in the Middle Ages | Includes index.
Identifiers: ISBN 9781499464726 (library bound)
Subjects: LCSH: Military art and science—History—Medieval, 500-1500—Juvenile literature. | Military history, Medieval—Juvenile literature.
Classification: LCC U37.B38 2017 | DDC 355.02'0940902—dc23

Manufactured in China

CONTENTS

Warfare has been a horrifying and destructive human activity since the dawn of history. Some people believe that modern war, with our ability to kill large numbers of people remotely with long-distance drones and weapons of mass destruction, is worse than it has ever been. Many tend to romanticize an earlier era of human conflict: the Middle Ages. Popular culture, including films, fantasy fiction, and television shows, often romanticize medieval warfare, even as they depict its brutality.

Europe during the medieval era was an often violent and brutal place. Primitive versions of explosive weapons and firearms were not widely used until nearly the end of the middle ages—that is, the historical era between the years 500 CE and 1500 CE.

Until then, war and combat were more personal. Even with large armies, the fighting was done mainly one on one, by infantry and warriors on horseback called cavalry. Enemy forces tried to kill each other with swords, knives, axes, maces, clubs, and similar hand weapons. From a distance, the bow and arrow, crossbow, and machines that hurled projectiles were the main tools people used to maim and kill their foes.

The story of medieval combat is one of both people and their inventions. Throughout the centuries, the quality of armor and weapons

This illustration, *Knights of the Holy Ghost Embarking for the Crusades*, is from a nineteenth-century manuscript on the Middle Ages. War was a common part of many medieval peoples' experience.

the talent of fighters, and the generals and other military leaders that decided on strategy were all major factors in who got the upper hand in battle. The defensive measures used in the design of castles and other fortifications, as well as the weapons used to overcome them, were also crucial. Eventually, the advent of ever more deadly guns, cannon, aircraft, and other inventions would make medieval weapons and warcraft obsolete. For now, though, let us take a look at how battle looked in Europe for nearly a millennium.

CHAPTER ONE

KNIGHTS AND MEDIEVAL CONFLICT

Many people imagine the era of struggles on the battlefield, castle sieges, and knights in shining armor as an exciting one, full of chivalry and heroism. In reality, such romantic notions fail to capture the horror and devastation that war has always brought to people, both to those who fight it and the innocent victims left behind.

Through the many museums, castles, monuments, paintings, tapestries, and other artifacts left behind, and the written accounts and scholarly works of all eras documenting them, we can trace back the history and development of medieval combat and imagine what it was truly like.

THE ROAD TO KNIGHTHOOD

During the early Middle Ages, the term "knight" simply referred to a soldier who went into battle on horseback.

As the art of warfare in medieval Europe developed, only the rich could afford to equip themselves with the latest weapons, armor, and suitable horses. Accordingly, knights almost always came from aristocratic and noble families.

Preparing to become a knight took many years of training. At the age of about seven, a boy from a noble family would be sent to live at the home of a relative or a neighboring knight. There he served as a page, waiting upon his master at the table and carrying out errands. In return, he was taught the first steps of fighting, using blunt wooden swords. He also learned to wrestle and ride a horse. Later he might practice jousting by charging at a quintain, which was a target at one end of an arm, mounted on a revolving post. If he was too slow, a weighted bag at the other end of the arm would swing around and knock him off his horse!

An illustration shows that a knight did not engage in a military career alone but was assisted by pages, squires, and groomsmen (those who cared for horses).

At the age of fourteen, a page was sent to another home or castle where he became a squire. The word "squire" comes from the French word *ecuyer*, meaning "shield-bearer." It was now his job to help a knight put on his armor before battle, and he would also assist a knight if he was injured or unhorsed. Squires were expected to be very fit. They spent long hours developing their sword and jousting skills. It was also important to learn the rules of chivalry, a code that defined how a knight was to behave in times of war and also at court during times of peace. The word "chivalry" is derived from the French word *chevalier*, meaning "horseman."

At the age of about twenty-one, a squire was ready to become a knight, but first it was usual to undergo a ceremony of purification. Often this involved a bath to wash away sins, which was followed by putting on colored robes to symbolize his new position—white for purity, red to show he was prepared to shed his blood for a just cause, and black to show that he was prepared to die. He then spent a night kneeling before the altar in church. The following morning, his sword was blessed and he took a vow "to fear God, serve the king, protect the weak, and live honorably." In full armor he then knelt in front of the king, who dubbed (or touched) the knight on the shoulder with the flat side of his sword.

FEUDALISM AND KNIGHTHOOD

In 1066, Duke William of Normandy, an area in northern France, conquered England at the Battle of Hastings. The story of the invasion is depicted on a tapestry that can still be seen in Bayeux, a small town in northern France. William rewarded the nobles who fought for him by giving them land. In return for these gifts of land, William demanded to be paid homage and to be given military service. This became known as the feudal system, from the Latin word *feudum*, meaning "land held." Each noble knelt before William, who was now king, and said: "I promise to become your man, to hold these lands faithfully and perform my due service." The king told his nobles they must

Hand-to-hand combat was common in medieval war. Here, English forces under King Harold fight off a force of Norwegian Vikings at close quarters during the Battle of Stamford Bridge in September 1066.

always be ready to fight for him, and he also told them how many knights they were expected to bring with them. Bishops were also granted land, and they, too, were expected to provide a certain number of knights when required. William was determined to keep a strong hold on the country he had conquered.

The number of knights each duke, baron, or bishop was expected to provide varied according to the amount of land he governed. The Normans anticipated

 ## COMPETING IN TOURNAMENTS

It took many years of training to become a knight, so it was important in times of peace to maintain the skills that had been acquired. Tournaments originated in northern France between about 1050 and 1070 and were an excellent way for a knight to prove he was fit for war.

Two types of events developed. The first was a mock free-for-all battle called a mêlée. This was sometimes held between knights from nearby castles, with the aim that one set of knights should capture and hold as many opposing knights as possible. Later, the winning side would ransom the knights it held. Watching knights fight in single combat soon became popular, and stands were specially constructed for the spectators.

In the later Middle Ages, jousting was probably the most spectacular event at a tournament. Jousting involved pairs of knights on horseback charging at each other with lances, which were usually blunted with crown-shaped ends called coronals. Knocking another knight off his horse became more difficult as higher-backed saddles were designed. Although a barrier separated horses so that head-on collisions were avoided, the force with which the lances struck and splintered often caused injury and sometimes death, despite the full body armor knights wore in later years.

At the height of their popularity in the thirteenth century, tournaments became as much a spectacle as they were a serious part of a knight's training. Tournaments were held over several days, and there were valuable prizes to be won, such as a new suit of armor or a warhorse. Each day, heralds announced who would be participating, identifying each knight by the symbols on his shield and surcoat. The top of a knight's helmet might feature a symbol from a coat of arms, such as a colorful animal.

Entertainment was provided in the evenings. Important guests would banquet and dance at the castle, providing the chance for romance between contestants and noble ladies. The next day, a knight might be granted the favor of a lady by wearing her scarf on his sleeve. This was also the age of courtly love!

11

resistance from the Englishmen they had subdued, and so a program of castle building was quickly undertaken. At first, these castles were made of wood, consisting of a stockade on a mound of earth. Gradually, these were replaced by impressive stone castles, which provided considerable protection for the occupants. Nevertheless, it was not long before William called upon his nobles for military support when faced by rebellion in the north of England during 1069.

Some nobles housed the knights they commanded in the castles they built. Other nobles granted knights their own estates of land, called manors. These knights were expected to swear homage to their local lord. However, William made sure all knights first swore allegiance to himself as king. He did not want to face rebellion from his lesser vassals. In each village, the peasants were expected to serve the knight who was their local lord. In times of war, this might mean going into battle carrying whatever makeshift weapons were available, if only a farm pitchfork.

MEDIEVAL MILITARY ORDERS

During the eleventh and twelfth centuries, several groups of military monks were founded. There were three main orders, as they were called: the Knights of St. John, the Knights Templar, and the Knights of the Teutonic Order. The knights who joined these orders took religious vows, promising to be poor, obedient, and chaste (meaning having no sexual relations with women). However, they also promised to use their military skills in holy wars and to protect fellow Christians.

This was the time of the Crusades. Muslim Saracens from the Middle East had captured Jerusalem and the area regarded by Christians in Europe as the Holy Land. In 1095, Pope Urban II called upon the kings and princes of Christian Europe to recapture Jerusalem. The word "crusade" comes from the Latin *crux*, meaning

Jousting in tournaments—like this one in the 1350s—began as a means of training knights and keeping their skills sharp, but it became an institution within medieval culture in its own right.

a cross, because the pope told warriors to sew a cloth cross onto their tunics as they went to war.

The Knights of St. John, founded in 1099 when the Christians captured Jerusalem, were also known as the Hospitallers because they kept a hospital in Jerusalem where they looked after the sick. The Knights Templar, also founded in 1099, took their name from their head-quarters on the Temple Mount in Jerusalem, where they swore allegiance to the patriarch of Jerusalem. The order grew rapidly in number and became very wealthy as admirers donated land in Europe to the knights in an effort to support their work. The Knights of the Teutonic Order originated in Germany and were founded in about 1190. They were also active in eastern Europe, where they helped to spread Christianity to areas in Poland, in Hungary, and near the Baltic Sea.

The knights in these orders devoted their lives to the defense of the Holy Land, particularly in the years between the Crusades. They built huge castles from which they rode out to protect pilgrims. When the Crusades came to an end, the orders spread to other areas of Europe, including Spain, where they fought against the Moors from North Africa, who occupied Spain until 1492.

CHAPTER TWO

TOOLS FOR WAR

When we think about knights, the weapon we likely most imagine is the sword. Of course, the manufacture of swords predates medieval knights by thousands of years. In the Bronze Age—beginning around 3300 BCE, and 3200 BCE in Europe—early swords were forged from bronze, though this made them soft compared to later ones. Much later, iron became the standard metal used in sword manufacture. The technique known as pattern-welding had been developed by the Middle Ages. This involved layering hard and soft iron rods alternately and then twisting and hammering them together. Harder rods were then hammer-welded onto the sword to provide the cutting edges. Blacksmiths (the artisans who made the swords) would then heat this metal in a furnace, and then plunge it into cold water. It then cooled naturally. This strengthened the sword. Finally, the sword was shaped and sharpened.

Because it took so long to make them, swords were expensive. Good swords were regarded as prize possessions by those who could afford them, principally knights. The best swords were passed on from one generation to the next. The Vikings from Scandinavia gave their swords names, such as Hvati (keen) or Langhrass (long and sharp), and this tradition carried on into the Middle Ages. Everyone knows that the sword of the legendary King Arthur was called Excalibur.

Between the handle and the blade, a sword had a quillion. This was usually a simple straight bar at right angles to the blade, providing protection to the hand. At the other end of the handle was a pommel, to help prevent loss of grip. The period when a sword was designed can be determined partly by the shape of the pommel, which was D-shaped at the start of the Middle Ages. Later, it was shaped like a Brazil nut, and later still, it became disc-shaped and was often mounted with a coat of arms. If a sword was used more for ceremony, its pommel might be inlaid with a precious stone and it was sheathed in a highly decorated metal scabbard. However, scabbards were usually made of leather and hung from a waist belt called a bawdrick.

The length and shape of swords changed during the Middle Ages. When chain mail was worn as the main form of protective armor, a typical sword was about three feet long and double-edged, with a fairly steep point. It could then be used for both slashing and stabbing. As plate armor developed, it was less effective to slash at an opponent, and so knights tried to thrust through chinks and weak spots between various pieces of armor. As a result, swords were made with a sharper, sloping point. Wearing plate armor also meant that knights relied less on protecting themselves by carrying a shield. With two hands free, swords increased in length to between four and five feet, sometimes with a fuller, or shallow groove, along the length of the blade, to help reduce the overall weight. Knights would use these massive swords to deliver crushing blows in an attempt to cause injury and to knock each other over. A

A series of swords is displayed inside the Great Hall in the famous Edinburgh Castle in Edinburgh, Scotland. The sword was the most basic and widely used weapon by medieval fighters.

short dagger, called a misericord, meaning "dagger of mercy," would also be carried, so a fallen foe might be dispatched quickly.

OTHER MEDIEVAL WEAPONS

In the early Middle Ages, knights on horseback charged at their enemies with a lance, which varied little from the spears used by ordinary foot soldiers. It was the use of a stirrup for the feet, an invention from the Far East, that allowed a knight to control his horse and balance himself on impact. Over the years, knights wore more extensive armor, and so bigger and stronger horses were used. In turn, this meant that much longer and heavier lances could be carried. They were now made from tree trunks, turned on a lathe, and made thicker. Sometimes armor featured a bracket on which to rest the lance for additional support.

After the impact of a charge, knights might continue to fight on horseback, at which point a ball and chain, a war hammer, an axe, or a mace might by used in preference to a sword. The ball and chain featured an iron ball covered in spikes, which was attached to a short shaft by a chain that was swung at arm's length to give the ball extra force on impact. More common was the war hammer. This had a fairly short shaft with a sharp spike on one side of the head that could pierce through plate armor. On the other side of the head there was a hammer used to dent armor so as to restrict movement. Axes varied in design. In the early Middle

Ages, they were huge, with long handles. A Danish or Saxon warrior swinging a large axe could easily knock off a man's head with one blow. Later, smaller axes with shorter shafts were used. The mace was a metal club with an enlarged or flanged head capable of delivering a powerful blow that could cause injury or concussion. Bishop Odo, half brother of William I of England, is shown on the Bayeux Tapestry waving a mace above his head. A bishop or priest was not allowed to spill blood with a sword, but battering one's enemies with a mace was obviously thought to be acceptable.

ARMOR

During the eleventh and twelfth centuries, knights wore chain mail made from rings of iron that were interlocked to form a shirt called a hauberk or byrnie. The armor came down as far as the knees, at which point it was split to make riding a horse easier. Underneath, a padded garment called an aketon helped to soften sword blows. Over time, the hauberk was extended to include iron sleeves, mittens, and a hood. Helmets were conical in shape and often had a wide nose guard at the front. The weight of all this chain mail was considerable. Knights also carried large, kite-shaped shields made of wood and covered with leather. These shields were slightly curved toward the body, were decorated on the front, and had carrying straps on the back.

The full head-to-toe covering provided by body armor was both effective in preventing injury but also unwieldy if a knight was unhorsed.

By the start of the thirteenth century, the great helm had been introduced to give a knight's face and head extra protection. This was a flat-topped, round-sided, metal box with narrow eye slits at the front. It was very heavy, so it was made long enough to rest on the shoulders, which helped bear its weight. Because the face was now completely covered, knights on the battlefield recognized each other by their coats of arms, painted on their shields and surcoats.

Plate armor started to appear in the fourteenth century. Knights had already experimented with body armor called cuir bouilli, which was made from leather. The leather was first boiled and then hardened into shape. Sometimes the leather was reinforced with small metal plates stitched into place. One piece covering the chest could be buckled to another on the back. However, plate armor was regarded as a better defense than leather against the increasing use of arrows in war. Single pieces of armor were shaped individually and strapped over chain mail, at first covering just the legs and arms.

As the techniques used to fashion armor developed, the helm was replaced by the bascinet, which was a more closely fitted helmet with rounded surfaces to deflect blows. A removable or hinged visor was fitted to make breathing easier, and padding was riveted inside for additional comfort. Chain-mail neck guards called aventails were attached to the bottom of the bascinet with threads. Gauntlets for the hands and sabatons for the feet were made with overlapping plates, and armor was constructed for the shoulders, elbows, and knees

These armored knights on horseback are shown in a detail from a fresco from 1140. Over the years, suits of armor became ever more elaborate but also sometimes heavier and harder to manage.

to allow for as much natural movement as possible. With such increased protection, the large, kite-shaped shields used earlier by the Normans were replaced by smaller, triangular shields, which were lighter but still slightly curved to hug the body. At the same time, the long surcoat was replaced by a shorter jupon, which still showed the coat of arms.

Simone IV de Montfort, pictured here in armor with sword and shield, was a French warlord famous for his participation in the Crusades.

A knight's warhorse was both extremely important and expensive. It was fitted with a cloth covering that bore the knight's coat of arms, but underneath, there was a layer of padding. In the later Middle Ages, armor was made especially for horses. At the very least, a horse would wear a shaffron to cover its head and nose, but sometimes more extensive armor would also cover its neck and sides.

The early fifteenth century found many important centers for the production of complete suits of armor, including Augsburg, Nuremberg, and Passau in Germany; Milan in Italy; Paris in France; and

Greenwich in England. Iron ore was needed, together with coal or charcoal, and some armorers also used waterpower to work heavy hammers and other simple machines. The ways in which different craftsmen worked were jealously guarded secrets, but the best suits of armor covered the entire body and allowed a knight to remain astonishingly nimble. The idea that a knight had to be winched up, hoisted, and lowered onto his horse is not true.

During the sixteenth century, the most expensive suits of armor copied the fashions of courtly clothing. German armor often looked as if it was made of pleated fabric, whereas Italian armor was generally smoother. Suits were painted black or were given a blue color during heating, while suits at the top end of the market were engraved with designs or even gilded with gold.

CHAPTER THREE

WARCRAFT

Europe during the early Middle Ages was dominated by feudalism, the social and political system in which nobles supporting a king or other ruler were granted land to own in exchange for their military loyalty and support. One rung down from the nobility were vassals, who were their tenants. Peasants, or serfs, lived on the land of the vassals and provided loyalty, labor, and a share of their agricultural production. In wartime, vassals were obligated to provide troops to the nobles above them, who in turn provided their military support to their monarchs.

During peacetime, there were few active-duty soldiers ready for battle, and usually monarchs set up alternate ways of providing support and loyalty. One example of this system working was in England in the twelfth century. In 1154 CE, Henry II took the crown after a period of civil war. Instead of providing soldiers, barons and other nobles paid Henry scutage, or shield money. This gradually became an annual tax. The king then would use this money to hire mercenaries (soldiers for hire)—for example, to fight conflicts in France.

King Edward I of England, who reigned from 1272 to 1307, fought a series of battles in Wales and Scotland. He needed troops for long periods of time and recruited them by means of what were called indentures. Once the king had agreed with a trusted nobleman how many troops he would provide and how much he would be paid, a clerk wrote out the details of the agreement twice, on a large piece of parchment. This was then cut into two pieces along a jagged line. The king kept one part of the parchment and the nobleman the other part. Both parties then had proof of their agreement because the two pieces of parchment would fit together like teeth. The in-denture derived its name from the French word *dent*, meaning "tooth."

FOOT SOLDIERS

By the fourteenth century, knights in an army were greatly outnumbered by foot soldiers and archers. For example, Edward I used 25,000 men-at-arms, or infantry, but only 5,000 horsemen in his campaigns against the Welsh and Scots. These troops wore iron helmets and aketons, or leather jackets, sometimes riveted with metal plates.

The foot soldier in the later Middle Ages often carried a sword and a dagger, but it was a weapon variously known as a pike, poleaxe, or halberd that made him so effective. These weapons combined the features of both the spear and the axe, giving foot soldiers the potential to defeat mounted knights. Indeed, Flemish pikemen at the Battle of Courtrai in 1302 defeated an army of French knights, killing over 1,000 of them. This was the first occasion that foot soldiers had scored such a victory. Soldiers also started to make limited use of firearms during the late fourteenth century.

In the Battle of Bannockburn, a conflict in June 1314, Scottish forces under Robert the Bruce defeated the English under Edward II, who had tried to relieve British troops besieged by the Scots at Stirling Castle nearby.

ARCHERS

It was the archers that knights feared most. The Bayeux Tapestry shows Norman archers using fairly short bows at the Battle of Hastings, but by the thirteenth century, the longbow was changing the way in which battles were fought. Edward I was the first monarch to realize the potential of the longbow when he saw it being used by the Welsh. The arrow, fired from a six-foot bow made of elm, was capable of piercing an oak door four inches thick. When fired over a distance, it was accurate up to about 200 yards (183 meters) and could reach up to 400 yards (366 meters).

It took great strength and skill to use the bow. Boys started to practice on smaller bows, and at one stage in England all male peasants were required by law to practice on their village green, shooting at targets called butts. An archer wore a bracer on the left wrist to provide support as he pulled the

English bowmen are shown in this illustration. Over time, archers would become far more decisive in medieval warfare, as arrows traveled farther.

bowstring, and on the right hand he wore a glove to protect the fingers. Arrows between 30 and 36 inches (76 and 91 centimeters) long had a pointed steel tip capable of penetrating chain mail. At short range, one of these steel-tipped arrows could also penetrate plate armor. Goose feathers were used at

 ## PREPARING FOR BATTLE

There were literally hundreds of battles fought throughout Europe during the Middle Ages, so readiness was important. Fletchers were kept busy producing arrows, craftsmen made armor, and there was a constant need to breed suitable horses and keep them well shod. If it was going to be a long campaign, or if an army was expected to travel abroad, then many people in addition to knights and soldiers would be off to war.

The English army would commandeer merchant ships if crossing the channel to fight in France. When it arrived, the army would need to be fed. Soldiers raided farms and peasant homes, carrying off whatever food they could find. Horses also needed to graze, and if possible, military activity was planned for the summer months when the grass was tall.

Surprise was often crucial. Spies may have been reporting information about the enemy for weeks or even months, but as a battle approached, small detachments of horsemen were sent to carry out reconnaissance. They needed to track the enemy and also look for a suitable battleground, as geographical advantage could make all the difference. Positioning your forces on a hill meant the enemy would have to attack by charging up a slope, or perhaps a wooded area might hide troops until they were required.

Opposing armies might camp quite close to each other for several days before a battle. At night, nobles and knights slept in tents while foot soldiers huddled around hundreds of campfires. During the day, soldiers might be ordered to cut down trees to prepare defensive stakes. Devices known as caltrops were spread over the ground on which the enemy would charge. These were made of metal and had four sharp prongs sticking out in different directions. When thrown down, they always landed with one prong pointing upward, causing injury if trodden on by a man or horse.

Nobles met to discuss their battle plans, and at some point a commander might send his herald to the enemy camp to offer peace terms. If one side greatly outnumbered the other, then perhaps the smaller army might be persuaded to turn back. However, a smaller force might have no other option than to fight. If there was time before a battle, a priest said prayers and troops would cross themselves. Then the king or commanding noble might give a rousing speech to encourage everyone on to victory.

the other end of the arrow to provide stability as it flew through the air.

The bow was strung before battle, and arrows were carried in a quiver worn on the hip. In battle, the arrows were usually stuck in the ground in front of the archer so they could be grabbed quickly. Standing in ranks, archers would fire wave after wave of arrows high in the air, causing injury and huge loss of life to enemy troops. Knights might be safe at a distance, but their horses would rear up and cause chaos when hit. If enemy knights charged, archers standing behind rows of sharpened stakes would wait until the knights were within range and then shoot with devastating accuracy.

The crossbow was very different in design and was favored by soldiers in most countries on mainland Europe. A much shorter and stiffer bow was mounted at the end of a wooden handle called a stock. The string on the bow was pulled back with a hook and held ready for firing by the nut, which was a notch in a revolving cylinder. A quarrel, or bolt, was then placed in a groove running along the length of the stock and was fired when the trigger released the nut. Crossbows could be used by relatively unskilled troops and were accurate and very powerful over quite a distance, though they lacked the range of the longbow. Later models used mechanical cranks to winch back the bowstring. The big disadvantage of the crossbow was the length of time it took to reload, whereas a skilled man with a longbow could shoot six or more arrows per minute.

THE HEAT OF BATTLE

Battles were noisy affairs with clashing weapons, shouting, and screaming. Troop maneuvers would be signaled by trumpets, and drumbeats accompanied the foot soldiers as they marched forward.

Tactics were often influenced by tradition, and there was almost a set order of battle suggesting when archers should fire and when knights were to charge. It is said that some commanders consulted manuals dating back to Roman times. Tradition also dictated that men of the same rank should fight each other, so knights would engage in individual combat while ranks of foot soldiers attacked each other. Sometimes these conventions were ignored. Henry V of England caused outrage during the Battle of Agincourt in 1415 when he gave his foot soldiers the signal to hack to death hundreds of knights stuck in the mud.

Defending the standard, or flag, was regarded as important, as it was a rallying point for troops. To lose a flag was a disgrace and would indicate that the enemy was winning. During the Crusades, Sir Richard

Alfonso II of Aragon and Alfonso VII of Castile during the siege of Cuenca, Spain, in 1177. The camp of their army is behind them.

The Battle of Agincourt in northern France, displayed in this artistic rendering, marked a decisive English military victory over France during the Hundred Years' War. It was notable for the extensive use of archers by the English, led by Henry V.

de Guise lost his left hand but fought on, holding his standard with a bloody stump. Beside him, the earl of Salisbury, William Longespée, lost a foot and both arms as he continued to defend the standard. They were both killed, having refused protection if they surrendered.

THE AFTERMATH

Victorious foot soldiers swiftly killed enemy troops lying injured and dying. Their own injured would be carried off using shields as stretchers. Heralds compiled lists of the dead, and soldiers stripped bodies of their weapons and armor and then pillaged local villages and towns. A knight who had been captured alive was held for ransom and spent months or even years in an enemy castle until his family paid for his release. Knights held as prisoners were usually treated with civility. During the twelfth century in France, a religious group called the Trinitarians was formed specifically to help negotiate the release of knights. In 1250, the French king was held ransom by Saracens during the Crusades. He was later released, after having surrendered the Egyptian city of Damietta and handing over a vast quantity of gold.

CHAPTER FOUR

FAMOUS MEDIEVAL BATTLES AND CAMPAIGNS

E xamining some famous battles of the medieval era can give us insight into the way warfare was truly waged during that time. This includes examining the reasons why certain military forces and their leadership prevailed, while others were defeated.

THE BATTLE OF HASTINGS, OCTOBER 14, 1066 CE

The Battle of Hastings marked a major milestone in English history. It was the first of and one of the most decisive battles of the invasion of the Normans in the eleventh century. One of the most important records of the events leading up to the eventual Norman conquest of England is found in the artifact known as the Bayeux Tapestry. *The Anglo-Saxon Chronicle*, a first-hand historical record of the era, also provides details about the conflict.

Hastings remains interesting to historians because the Saxons in England and the Normans from France utilized different weapons and military tactics. The Normans' triumph meant irrevocable changes in the governance of England. It would also closely link the fates and histories of France and England for the next few centuries. A number of military conflicts would arise as a result.

This painting shows the Battle of Hastings, which took place October 14, 1066, and marked a decisive Norman victory in their conquest of England.

Edward the Confessor, the Saxon king of England, died in 1066. He left no heir, and so England's most powerful noble, Harold Godwinson, was crowned. However, across the channel Duke William of Normandy claimed that both Edward and Harold had promised him the throne. He immediately prepared an army and a large fleet.

The king of Norway also claimed the throne and landed in northern England during the summer of 1066. Harold defeated him at Stamford Bridge, near York, before hearing that William had arrived on the south coast. Tired but determined, Harold marched his army south again.

The Bayeux Tapestry shows that the Normans were well organized. They brought with them everything they needed, including horses for their knights and even a prefabricated wooden fort. Having landed, they set about gathering food, but William knew he had to win a decisive battle soon, so he set about burning local villages, hoping that Harold would hurry all the faster to defend his kingdom.

The Saxons took up a good defensive position behind a shield wall on Senlac Hill, near Hastings. Their most experienced troops were the housecarls, armed with huge double-headed axes. They fought with great heroism, as if rooted to the ground. In contrast, the more sophisticated style of warfare used by the Normans demanded organized battle tactics and the controlled use of troops.

At first, the Normans at the foot of the hill tried to break up the Saxon ranks by using archers. Then their knights, armed with spears, charged, although the effort of climbing the hill must have been considerable. For several hours, the Saxons withstood the showers of arrows and the charge of the knights, but then came the turning point in the battle. Some less experienced Saxon soldiers thought they saw Norman knights in retreat and left their hilltop position to give chase. Was this a Norman trick? Disorganized and on foot, the Saxons were easily killed by the Norman knights and soldiers waiting at the bottom of the hill.

The tide of the battle turned further when Harold was killed. The Bayeux Tapestry shows that he was struck in the eye by an arrow and then hacked down by knights. His mutilated body was later placed under a pile of stones on the cliffs near Hastings, and only after many years was he given a proper burial at Waltham Abbey, north of London. William meanwhile marched to London, where he was crowned on the twenty-fifth of December.

THE BATTLE OF COURTRAI, "THE BATTLE OF THE GOLDEN SPURS," JULY 11, 1302

For much of the Middle Ages, a charge by knights on horseback was decisive in many battles. In Italy, for example, knights reigned supreme. However, the Battle of Courtrai showed that organized foot soldiers were capable of defeating such an enemy.

The Battle of the Golden Spurs (also known as the Battle of Courtrai) pitted the kingdom of France against rebelling Flemish forces.

Philip IV of France incorporated Flanders into his kingdom in 1300. This was a wealthy land covering roughly the same area as modern-day Belgium. The occupation and the unfair taxes that Philip imposed encouraged the people of Flanders to rise in rebellion. In 1302, the people of Bruges killed a number of French knights, and Philip decided to send an army to stamp out further rebellion.

On July 8, the French, led by Robert Artois, arrived at the Flemish town of Courtrai. Their army numbered 6,500 and included 2,500 knights. The Flemish army opposing them numbered 9,000 but consisted of only foot soldiers. Apart from about 400 nobles, they were mostly untrained craftsmen and peasants, led by Pieter de Coninck.

The French held a council of war. Although outnumbered, they decided to teach their enemy a lesson with a full frontal charge. The Flemish troops expected this and so they positioned themselves behind two brooks and an area of marshy ground, which some

THE BATTLE OF MORGARTEN

It was generally accepted, and remains so, that greater numbers are usually an advantage in any battle, whether by the standards of conventional warfare, or those of medieval warcraft. However, on November 15, 1315, it was a much smaller force that overtook a larger one in the Battle of Morgarten, which took place alongside Lake Ägerisee in what is now Switzerland. Tensions had arisen between the Austrians of the Holy Roman Empire and members of the Swiss Confederacy over the rights to certain lands bordering or belonging to the Swiss.

The Swiss numbered about 1,500 and used the element of surprise to ambush the Austrians, led by Leopold I, Duke of Austria, who commanded as many as 5,500 infantry and 2,500 cavalry. The assault began with the Swiss raining down rocks and logs onto the Austrians, after the latter entered a narrow part of a mountain pass between a steep incline and an impassable swamp.

Certainly, the terrain favored the well-trained and native Swiss, while it proved a distinct disadvantage to cavalry. The Swiss used their favored weapons, halberds, to overwhelm the Austrian cavalry. Many more ended up drowning in their panicked escape across the lake. Perhaps 1,500 Austrians perished, with many of their foot soldiers fleeing in retreat.

reports say they disguised with brushwood. In their arrogance, the French forgot to carry out the usual reconnaissance. Many of the knights managed to jump their horses successfully across the brooks, whereupon they became stuck in the boggy ground beyond. The Flemish troops had been told not to take any prisoners and so they slaughtered the stranded knights with pikes.

After the battle, 500 gold spurs were stripped from the French knights and taken to the Church of Our Lady in Courtrai. There they adorned a vault until the French reclaimed them when they defeated a Flemish army in 1382. The Battle of Courtrai was significant because the people of Flanders regained their independence. They also inspired other ordinary foot soldiers to take on massed ranks of knights. The Scots, for example, were standing behind a burn, or brook, when they defeated English knights at the Battle of Bannockburn in 1314.

THE BATTLE OF SLUYS, JUNE 24, 1340

The famous sea battle fought at Sluys came at the beginning of a long series of battles fought between England and France from 1337 to 1453, which later came to be known as the Hundred Years' War. Since the Battle of Hastings in 1066, English monarchs had ruled vast amounts of land in France, and the Hundred Years' War was really a struggle between the two countries over which areas they would each control. The wine-growing area of Bordeaux, for example, was especially valued for the trade it produced, and the city of Bordeaux itself was held by the English until 1453.

On June 24, 1340, Edward III of England set off toward Flanders (the home country of his wife) with a large army carried by a fleet of about 200 ships. As he approached the port of Sluys, a French fleet was seen, drawn up in defensive formation, with ships tied together in several lines. Their aim was to prevent the English from landing. Edward ordered

The naval Battle of Sluys between England and France, in which the English prevailed, is depicted in this miniature from a medieval manuscript. Naval battles became more and more important at the end of the middle ages.

his fleet to maneuver so that the wind and the sun were behind them.

The English ships had wooden battlements, or towers, at the front of each vessel, called the bow. As the English fleet came within range, archers equipped with longbows fired from these forecastles, as they were called, killing hundreds of French soldiers and sailors and giving the English the upper hand early in the battle. When the enemy ships came alongside each other, grappling irons were thrown, pulling the ships tightly together. Furious hand-to-hand fighting took place on the decks, while high up in crow's nests, soldiers hurled down huge stones, attempting to sink enemy ships.

This was certainly one of the bloodiest battles of the Middle Ages, partly because at sea there was no hope of escape. In addition to losing a large number of ships, about 18,000 French soldiers were killed, while English losses were relatively few. From then on, raids across the channel were unhindered, and English bowmen continued to be crucial during the Hundred Years' War, winning further victories at Crécy in 1346 and Poitiers in 1356. Perhaps the most famous victory won by archers was at Agincourt in 1415, when the French lost thousands of men and the English only a few hundred.

THE BATTLE OF BOSWORTH, AUGUST 22, 1485

The Battle of Bosworth concluded the Wars of the Roses—the thirty-year struggle between the nobles of the houses of York and Lancaster for control of the English throne—and brought the Middle Ages to a close in England. What is of particular interest is that until very late in the battle either side could have won. The balance was held by 6,000 soldiers who waited on one side of the field as their commander, Lord Stanley, made up his mind which side to support.

King Richard III was a controversial figure who commanded loyalty from many but was hated by others. He grabbed the English crown by allegedly murdering his two young nephews, both of whom were before him in

Toward the very end of the medieval era, the Battle of Bosworth on August 22, 1485, depicted here, marked the end of the English civil war known as the Wars of the Roses.

line of succession to the throne. Eventually, Richard was challenged by Henry Tudor, who also claimed the crown. Henry had been in exile in France, but when he landed in Wales with just 2,000 men, he marched east, gathering more troops as he went.

The two sides met at Bosworth, near Leicester. Richard arrived first and arranged his troops on Ambion Hill. He was supported by the duke of Norfolk, while Henry was supported by the earl of Oxford. Richard also expected Lord Stanley to support him, but the situation was delicate because Stanley was Henry Tudor's stepfather. As a precaution, Richard took Stanley's own son, Lord Strange, as a hostage. If Stanley did not support Richard, his son would be executed. But Lord Stanley saw that if he supported Richard, and Henry were to win, he would be out of favor with the new king. He therefore waited to see how the battle developed.

Suspecting Stanley's treachery, Richard led a group of knights in a brave charge straight at Henry. If Richard could kill his enemy, the battle would be over. It was now that Stanley ordered his troops into battle, to make sure of Henry's victory. Richard immediately ordered Lord Strange's execution, but his guards decided to release him, seeing that this would put them in a better position if Henry won the battle. Richard was the last English king to die in battle. He was taken off to be buried at Leicester, slumped naked over the back of a horse. Meanwhile, on the battlefield, Lord Stanley crowned his stepson, who became Henry VII.

CHAPTER FIVE

CASTLES AND SIEGE TACTICS

One of the most important and common sites of conflict during the Middle Ages was the castle. Castles served as not only the headquarters of noble families but also as bases from which they could launch attacks and military campaigns. Most important, their construction provided safety and defenses for the nobles, soldiers, and surrounding citizens escaping from enemy attacks. For these reasons, they were constructed all throughout Europe and were the most impressive buildings of their time, along with cathedrals.

DEFENSE OF A CASTLE

The earliest castles during the Middle Ages were of motte and bailey construction. A mound of earth was made, on which was built a small wooden tower, or keep, which was protected by a wall of wooden stakes.

Around the motte was another wall of stakes enclosing an area in which there were living quarters and store-rooms. A ditch surrounded the whole site.

Motte and bailey castles were gradually replaced by stronger stone castles, which were less vulnerable to fire. The enormous weight of stone keeps meant that they could not be built on an artificial mound, so castles were often built on natural rocky hills. Where this was not possible, extra protection might be given by diverting a river to create a moat filled with water around the castle.

This painted montage depicts the French siege of Mortagne, near Bordeaux, France, held by the British. On the center right side, a famous mercenary fighting for the French, Owen of Wales, is shown felled by an arrow, supposedly by an English double agent.

The square corners of stone keeps could be badly damaged by rocks hurled by catapults and siege machines, so round keeps and outer curtain walls started to appear by the mid-thirteenth century. Missiles glanced off their smooth surfaces. Later still, rings of two or even three concentric outer walls were built.

Castles became more and more ingenious in their design. The entrance was always a weak spot and so would be protected by a drawbridge. A sliding iron gate called a portcullis could be lowered over the entrance itself. Then there would often be a short tunnel before another portcullis. Any attackers trapped in the tunnel would have boiling pitch or water poured on them through holes in the roof. Another protection for the entrance was the barbican, a kind of three-sided tower raised over an open alleyway.

The tops of walls were given crenellations or parapets from behind which arrows could be fired. Ledges were built jutting out from the battlements for defenders to drop rocks or fend off siege ladders. The bases of castle walls sloped outward, so rocks dropped from above bounced off horizontally toward the enemy. Windows were narrow slits when viewed from outside, but inside they widened sharply to allow archers to fire in all directions. If attackers did manage to breach the entrance to a castle, they would have little hope of going any farther. Even spiral stairs were designed so that only a soldier coming down or retreating in defense could swing a sword.

At the first sign of danger, extra supplies would be brought within castle walls, including local farm animals. Any crops not harvested might be burned to prevent them being used by enemy troops. When an army arrived to besiege a castle, heralds would meet to negotiate. If the inhabitants did not agree to surrender at this stage, they could expect no mercy later if the castle was captured. A siege could last for many months or even years. Defenders were left hoping that a relief army would arrive, but meanwhile felt cut off from the outside world. During the Crusades, Turks used carrier pigeons to send and receive messages when besieged. In response, the European soldiers used birds of prey trained to kill other birds. Conditions in the castle would meanwhile decline rapidly. The spread of illness and disease was a constant fear, water supplies ran low, and when food was short the occupants would search for rats to eat.

ATTACKING A CASTLE

As the defense of castles became more effective, the methods of attack became increasingly more ingenious. Starving a castle into surrender might take a very long time, but at least it was relatively safe. On the other hand, attacking a castle directly was very dangerous. Any town near a castle would probably fall quite quickly. Burning arrows would set fire to thatched houses, while troops used battering rams on gates and scaled walls on long ladders. Much larger siege machines were needed to breach castle walls.

A besieging army might arrive with giant cross-bows and catapults in pieces, which would be recon-structed on site. Ballistas were used to fire large metal bolts, and mangonels threw boulders from an arm shaped like a large spoon. Ropes at one end of the arm were twisted to provide tension, while the other end was held fast and loaded just before release. Both of these weapons dated back to Roman times and were of limited effectiveness.

More terrifying was the trebuchet. This was a truly enormous catapult, capable of hurling stones weigh-ing between 100 and 200 pounds (45 and 90 kilo-grams) over several hundred yards. At one end of a long arm was a large container filled with rocks that acted as a counterbalance. At the other end of the arm was a sling, which whipped around in the air to give extra propulsion to the missile before its release. King Edward I of England ordered a trebuchet to be built during his campaign against Scotland. It was called Warwolf, and with an arm about fifty feet (fif-teen meters) long, it threw boulders with such force that they penetrated castle walls.

Catapults were also used to throw diseased an-imal carcasses into castles in an effort to spread dis-ease. Between 1097 and 1098, it took a crusading army eight months to capture the Turkish-held city of Antioch (now Antakya). During the siege, 200 decapitated Turkish heads were catapulted into the castle in an attempt to demoralize the defenders. Eventually, an armorer turned traitor and opened the gates. Elsewhere, there were stories that enemy

THE SIEGE OF ACRE

Some of the most notable battles of the medieval era did not take place in Europe. As noted earlier, the Crusaders from Europe not only made expeditions to the Middle East to defend sites they considered part of the holy territory of Christendom but also to defend Christian pilgrims to the Holy Land in the area of Palestine.

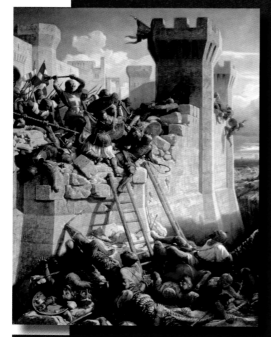

One pivotal battle occurred at the Crusader-controlled walled fortress city of Acre (now in northern Israel) beginning in early April 1291. In this case, the Mamluk Sultanate, commanded by Al-Ashraf Kalil, had besieged members of the Kingdom of Jerusalem, the Christian Crusader state that claimed the region, and members of the military orders known as the Knights Templar, the Knights Hospitaller, and the Teutonic Knights.

Kalil used powerful siege engines and thousands of volunteers, with some estimates

Guillaume de Clermont defends the walls at the Siege of Acre in 1291 (now in Israel), one of the more important battles of the era, fought between Crusaders and the Mamluk Sultanate.

putting the number of the Sultanate's forces at between 160,000 and 220,000, while the besieged crusaders numbered only about 18,000. Over the course of more than six weeks, the attackers' catapults weakened the walls of the city. Thousands of arrows were shot by the Muslim forces. The defenders were forced to retreat to the city's inner walls by May 16. Finally, even those defenses were breached, and many knights escaped in the chaos, but the city was defeated, its inhabitants slain or enslaved.

heralds were put into catapults and sent flying back into the castle grounds!

Another technique used to gain entry to a castle involved filling the moat with earth and stones to allow a siege tower to be pushed up against a castle wall. The siege tower was a tall wooden construction on wheels, covered on the outside by animal hides that were soaked in water to prevent the tower from being set on fire. Soldiers climbed up ladders inside the tower and then over a drawbridge and onto the castle battlements. A huge, metal, pointed battering ram, suspended under a roof, could also be pushed on wheels up to a gate. Rocks thrown from above made this a hazardous operation, but archers standing behind wicker fences tried to shoot defenders on the castle walls.

Perhaps the most time-consuming way to break into a castle involved mining underneath the castle

One of the most fearsome weapons of the medieval era was the battering ram. It was employed against both defensive walls and gates, and was a vital weapon until cannons and explosives made it obsolete.

walls by digging a tunnel supported by wood posts. When the tunnel was completed, it was filled with branches and then set on fire. The aim was to bring down the castle wall as the posts shoring up the tunnel collapsed.

CANNONS AND GUNS

Gunpowder, a mixture of saltpeter, sulfur, and charcoal, was probably discovered first in China. Knowledge of its use spread west to the Arab world and then to Europe, where the earliest illustration of a cannon, called a bombard, dates from 1327. The first cannons were made from strips of metal bound together by hoops, making them quite dangerous to use. As late as 1460, King James II of Scotland was killed while standing too close to a cannon that exploded. Later cannons were made of cast metal. Their range was further improved by the development of better gunpowder in granule form, and safer ways of firing cannons were also devised.

At first, cannons were used in sieges rather like catapults, merely to fire rocks. Soon metal balls were found to be more effective, and cannons were able to end a siege in a matter of weeks. In the mid-fifteenth century, thanks to the increasing effectiveness of cannons, the French drove the English from France as they quickly recaptured English-held castles. At about the same time, the kings of northern Spain drove the Moors from their castles in southern Spain.

Castles themselves were now being redesigned to cope with this new threat. Battlements were being strengthened, and castles were also mounting cannons on their walls. As early as 1381, Bologna in Italy had thirty-five cannons. It was difficult to use cannons in open battle, partly because they were so heavy to transport. Nevertheless, they certainly caused fear. Early muskets were also of limited use in battle because they were difficult to hold when fired. They operated like miniature cannons and had special hooks to fit over walls to cope with the recoil when

The English siege of Calais, France, lasted nearly a year, from September 1346 until August 1347, when French defenders were starved to the point of surrender.

fired. They gradually improved and became more effective, but at first they were best used in siege warfare.

The increasing use of cannons and firearms changed the pattern of warfare and helped to bring the Middle Ages to a close. Once masses of common infantrymen possessed firearms that could penetrate armor and bring down mounted horsemen at a distance of several hundred yards, the whole reason for the existence of a privileged caste of warrior knights disappeared, and along with them their code of valor and individual combat. The change began with the appearance of the Welsh longbow, and by the time reliable firearms were introduced, the glory was disappearing from the battlefield.

GLOSSARY

aketon Padded jacket worn by knights and foot soliders under chain mail to help soften sword blows.

ball and chain A metal ball covered in spikes and attached by a short chain to a wooden shaft.

ballista Giant crossbow, used for firing large arrows during sieges.

barbican A protected approach to a city or castle gate, consisting of an open alley surrounded by a three-sided tower.

bascinet A close-fitting helmet with round surfaces to deflect sword blows.

battering ram A tree trunk or wooden beam with a metal-tipped end, used for battering down castle and city gates.

battlements The raised parapets at the tops of castle walls, designed to protect against enemy projectiles.

bawdrick A waist belt from which a sword was hung.

bombard An early type of cannon.

butt A round target used for archery practice.

byrnie Chain mail shirt, also called a hauberk.

caltrop A piece of twisted iron with four small, sharp prongs, thrown down on the ground before battles to inflict injury to men and horses.

chain mail A form of flexible armor made of interlocking iron rings

concentric walls Rings of defensive walls around castles.

crenellations The defensive battlements on a castle wall, used to provide shelter for protection, with openings for firing arrows.

curtain wall The outer defensive wall of a castle.

drawbridge Bridge that could be lowered over a moat or ditch.

fletcher A person who makes arrows.

gauntlet A protective glove made of armor.

halberd A long pole with a metal spear and axe at one end.

hauberk A shirt made of chain-mail armor.

herald High-ranking servant who acted as a messenger and who also organized tournaments.

mangonel A type of catapult used when laying siege to a castle.

mercenary A soldier for hire, often originating from another country.

misericord A dagger used to kill wounded knights.

pike A long pole with a metal spear and axe or hook at one end.

pillage The act of raiding a place after battle to steal valuables.

quintain A revolving target used to practice jousting skills.

quiver A holder for arrows, worn over the shoulder or on a belt.

sabaton Protective armor used on the feet.

scutage A tax paid to the king instead of providing troops for battle.

surcoat A cloth coat-of-arms worn over chain mail.

trebuchet A siege weapon with a long arm that threw large rocks.

visor The removable front of a knight's helmet.

Canadian Society of Medievalists
c/o Roisin Cossar
Department of History
University of Manitoba
454 Fletcher Argue Building
Winnipeg, MB R3T 5V5
Website: http://www.canadianmedievalists.ca
The Canadian Society of Medievalists is an academic
   organization dedicated to promoting excellence in
   research for all aspects of medieval studies.

Columbia University Medieval Colloquium
602 Philosophy Hall
Columbia University
New York, NY 10027
Website: http://blogs.cuit.columbia.edu/medguild
The Medieval Colloquium (formerly the Medieval
   Guild) of Columbia University is a graduate stu-
   dent organization for medievalists whose mission
   is to help students develop professionally in their
   research about this historical period.

International Center of Medieval Art (ICMA)
The Cloisters, Fort Tryon Park
99 Margaret Corbin Drive
New York, NY 10040
(212) 928-1146
Website: http://www.medievalart.org
The International Center of Medieval Art promotes and

supports the study, understanding, and preservation of the visual and material cultures of medieval Europe, including the Mediterranean region and the Slavic world.

Medieval Academy of America
17 Dunster Street, Suite 202
Cambridge, MA 02138
(617) 491-1622
Website: http://www.medievalacademy.org
The Medieval Academy of America is the largest organization in the United States promoting excellence in medieval studies, including fostering research, publication, and teaching in medieval art, archaeology, history, law, literature, music, philosophy, religion, science, and social and economic institutions.

Rocky Mountain Medieval and Renaissance Association
c/o Jennifer McNabb
Department of History
Western Illinois University
438 Morgan Hall
1 University Circle
Macomb, IL 61455
E-mail: Jl-mcnabb@wiu.edu
Website: http://www.rmmra.org
The Rocky Mountain Medieval and Renaissance Association is a nonprofit, academic organization dedicated to the advancement of learning in the fields of medieval and Renaissance studies.

Society for Creative Anachronism (SCA)
PO Box 360789
Milpitas, CA 95036
(408) 263-9305
Website: http://www.sca.org
The Society for Creative Anachronism is an international organization dedicated to researching and re-creating the arts and skills of pre-seventeenth century Europe.

WEBSITES

Because of the changing nature of internet links, Rosen Publishing has developed an online list of websites related to the subject of this book. This site is updated regularly. Please use this link to access the list:

http://www.rosenlinks.com/LMID/weapon

FOR FURTHER READING

Bachrach, Bernard S., and David Bachrach. *Warfare in Medieval Europe c. 400-c. 1453*. New York, NY: Routledge, 2016

Bartlett, Clive. *English Longbowmen 1330–1515*. Oxford, UK: Osprey Publishing, 2002.

Cootes, Richard John. *The Middle Ages*. New York, NY: Longman, 1996.

Dougherty, Martine. *Medieval Warrior: Weapons, Technology, and Fighting Techniques, AD 1000-1500*. Guilford, CT: Lyons Press, 2011.

Gravett, Christopher. *Knights at Tournament*. Oxford, UK: Osprey Publishing, 1988.

Guard, Timothy. *Chivalry, Kingship and Crusade* (Warfare in History). Woodbridge, UK: Boydell Press, 2016.

Hill, Paul. *The Norman Commanders: Masters of Warfare 911-1135*. Barnsley, UK: Pen & Sword Books, 2013.

Janin, Hunt, and Ursula Carson. *Mercenaries in Medieval and Renaissance Europe*. Jefferson, NC: McFarland, 2013.

Jones, Robert W. *Bloodied Banners: Martial Display on the Medieval Battlefield* (Warfare in History). Woodbridge, UK: Boydell Press, 2015.

Langley, Andrew. *Castle at War*. London, UK: Dorling Kindersley, 1998.

Steele, Philip. *The Medieval World*. London, UK: Kingfisher, 2000.

BIBLIOGRAPHY

Gravett, Christopher. *Knights at Tournament.* Oxford, UK: Osprey Publishing, 1988.

Guest, Ken, and Denise Guest. *British Battles*. London, UK: HarperCollins, 1997.

Hogg, Ian V. *The Encyclopedia of Weaponry*. London, UK: Greenwich Editions, 1998.

Hook, Richard, and Christa Hook. *Medieval Siege Warfare*. Oxford, UK: Osprey Publishing, 1990.

Jones, John. *The Medieval World*. Walton on Thames, UK: Thomas Nelson Ltd., 1979.

Matthew, Donald. *Atlas of Medieval Europe*. Oxford, UK: Phaidon Press Ltd., 1983.

Norman, Vesey. *Arms and Armour*. London, UK: Octopus Books, 1972.

Parker, Geoffrey. *Warfare*. Cambridge, UK: Cambridge University Press, 2000.

Rothero, Christopher. *Medieval Military Dress*. Poole, UK: Blandford Press, 1983.

Seymour, William. *Battles in Britain*. London, UK: Book Club Associates, 1979.

Wilkinson, Frederick. *Arms and Armour*. London, UK: Chancellor Press, 1978.

INDEX

A

Acre, Siege of, 50–51
Agincourt, Battle of, 31, 42
archers, 25, 27–30, 36
armor, 4, 6, 7, 8, 11,
    16–17, 18, 19–23
axe, 4, 18–19

B

ball and chain, 18
Bannockburn, Battle of, 40
Bayeux Tapestry, 9, 19,
    27, 34, 36, 37
Bosworth, Battle of, 42–44
bow and arrow, 4, 27–30

C

cannons, 5, 53–54
castles
  attacking of, 48–52
  defense of, 47–48
  types/construction of,
      12, 45–47
chivalry, 6, 8
Courtrai, Battle of, 26,
    37–40

crossbow, 4, 30, 49
Crusades, 13–14, 31,
    33, 48, 50

E

Edward I, 25, 27, 49
Edward III, 41–42
Edward the Confessor, 36

F

feudal system, 9, 24
firearms, 4, 5, 26, 53–54
foot soldiers, 18, 25–26,
    29, 31, 33, 37, 38,
    39, 40

G

Godwinson, Harold, 36,
    37
gunpowder, 52–53

H

Hastings, Battle of, 8, 27,
    34–37, 40
Henry II, 24

ABOUT THE AUTHORS

Margaux Baum is a writer and editor from Queens, New York.

Paul Hilliam is a graduate of London University. He is senior master at Derby Grammar School in England, where he enjoys teaching history and religious studies. He has traveled throughout Europe, the Middle East, and India, visiting sites of historical interest.

PHOTO CREDITS

Designer: Michael Moy; Editor: Philip Wolny; Photo Researcher: Philip Wolny